The Technology of Farming

Producing
Dairy and Eggs

Jane Bingham

Chicago, Illinois

www.capstonepub.com
Visit our website to find out more information about Heinemann-Raintree books.

To order:
☎ Phone 888-454-2279
🖱 Visit www.capstonepub.com to browse our catalog and order online.

Edited by Abby Colich, Megan Cotugno, and Nancy Dickmann
Designed by Victoria Allen
Picture research by Elizabeth Alexander
Illustrations by Oxford Designers and Illustrators

Originated by Capstone Global Library Ltd
Printed and bound in China by China Translation and Printing Services Ltd

16 15 14 13 12
10 9 8 7 6 5 4 3 2 1

Library of Congress Cataloging-in-Publication Data
Bingham, Jane.
 Producing dairy and eggs / Jane Bingham.—1st ed.
    p. cm.—(The technology of farming)
 Includes bibliographical references and index.
 ISBN 978-1-4329-6406-1 (hb)—ISBN 978-1-4329-6413-9 (pb)
1. Dairy farming—Juvenile literature. 2. Eggs—Production—Juvenile literature. I. Title. II. Series: Technology of farming.
 SF239.B615 2012
 636.2'142—dc23   2011037497

Acknowledgments
We would like to thank the following for permission to reproduce photographs: Alamy: pp. 17 (©North Wind Picture Archives), 19 (©Danita Delimont), 32 (©Peter Horree), 33 (©Paris Market), 37 (©Tim Scrivener), 43 (© Nick Turner); Corbis: pp. 7 (© Wu Hong/epa), 35 (© Layne Kennedy); Getty Images: pp. 9 (Dagli Orti), 11 (Jean-Francois Millet/The Bridgeman Art Library), 13 (Wallace Kirkland/Time Life Pictures), 14 (Lewis W. Hine/George Eastman House), 15 (Universal History Archive), 25 (Chien-min Chung), 31 (Bloomberg News/ Chris Warde-Jones); Photolibrary: pp. 18, 20, 34, 41; Shutterstock: pp. 4 (© gillmar), 6 (© Nadezhda Bolotina), 27 (© oznuroz), 30 (© Magone), 39 (© Igumnova Irina), 40 (© Sveta San).

Cover photo of milking of cows in a modern milking plant reproduced with permission from Photolibrary (CNS CNS/ Sinopictures).

Every effort has been made to contact copyright holders of any material reproduced in this book. Any omissions will be rectified in subsequent printings if notice is given to the publisher.

Disclaimer
All the Internet addresses (URLs) given in this book were valid at the time of going to press. However, due to the dynamic nature of the Internet, some addresses may have changed, or sites may have changed or ceased to exist since publication. While the author and publisher regret any inconvenience this may cause readers, no responsibility for any such changes can be accepted by either the author or the publisher.

Contents

Some words appear in the text in bold, **like this**. You can find out what they mean by looking in the glossary.

How Are Dairy and Eggs Produced?

The word "dairy" is used to describe milk and other foods made from milk. Cream, butter, cheese, and yogurt are all **dairy products**. Most of the dairy products that we eat and drink come from cows.

The average dairy cow produces around 6 or 7 gallons (22 to 26 liters) of milk a day. That's about 100 glasses of milk!

From the cow to you

Most dairy farmers in **developed countries** rely on **technology**. They use machines to milk their cows, and the milk is collected in a tanker, which is a truck with a very large refrigerated tank. The tanker transports the milk to a special factory known as a dairy **plant**.

At the dairy plant, the milk is **processed** to make sure it is safe to drink. Then it is poured into cartons, bottles, or other containers. The full milk containers are packed into refrigerated trucks, which carry them to shops and supermarkets. In some places milk is delivered directly to people's homes.

Modern technology

Dairy plants today use the latest technology to produce a range of dairy foods. This book will describe the methods and machines used in modern dairy plants. You can also find out how dairy foods were produced in the past.

Traditional methods

Some farmers in developing countries use very little technology. They milk their animals by hand, and they produce cheese and other products with the help of very simple tools and machines. These farmers use traditional methods that have been practiced for thousands of years.

Not just cows

Dairy products do not always come from cows. Many people enjoy goat's cheese. In Italy mozzarella cheese is made from buffalo milk. In Greece feta cheese is usually made from sheep milk. In some parts of the world, people drink milk from yaks and camels and make cheese and yogurt from it.

Eggs as well

This book discusses eggs as well as dairy products. Most of the eggs we eat are laid by hens (female chickens), but some people like to eat the eggs of geese, ducks, or quail. In parts of Africa, people eat guinea fowl eggs.

For many farmers today, egg production is big business. Some egg producers in the United States keep many millions of hens. Eggs are usually processed and packed in an egg processing plant.

People of the Ural Mountains drink reindeer milk!

These free-range hens can move around where they want to.

Intensive or organic?

All modern farmers use technology, but some farmers use **intensive farming** methods in order to make their animals produce as much as possible. Most intensive farmers run large-scale farms, with a lot of machinery. They often feed their animals specially prepared food to make them more **productive**. Intensive farmers produce large quantities of food, but some people think that this type of farming can have a bad effect on the animals.

Other farmers take a different approach. They believe that cows and hens should only eat natural food and should not be given certain medicines when they are ill. They also make sure their animals have plenty of freedom to **roam** outside. This method of farming is sometimes known as **organic farming**. You can find out more about intensive and organic farming in this book.

How Did Dairy Farming Begin?

People have been milking animals for at least 10,000 years. Around 8000 BCE groups of nomads (wandering people) in central Asia began keeping herds of sheep and goats. These animals produced milk as well as providing wool, meat, and skins. About the same time, farmers in the Middle East began to tame wild cattle. At first the cattle were mainly used as working animals, but around 3000 BCE Arab farmers started keeping dairy herds.

Learning to make cheese

Nobody knows when people first began making cheese, but there is an ancient legend that an Arab shepherd was the first cheese-maker. According to the legend, the shepherd was carrying milk in a sheep's stomach when he discovered that the milk had turned into solid cheese. A substance called **rennet**, which is found in the stomachs of all animals, had **reacted** with the milk to form cheese.

Ancient dairy farmers

The ancient Sumerians farmed in the Middle East from around 5000 to 2000 BCE. They kept cows and goats for their milk and cheese and stored their cheese in tall pottery jars. The ancient Egyptians were also expert cheese-makers. In ancient Egypt, dairy products were mainly enjoyed by the wealthy.

This ancient Egyptian tomb painting shows a farmer milking a dairy cow. It dates from around 2000 BCE.

Greeks and Romans

Farmers in ancient Greece kept sheep and goats for their milk and cheese. They made soft cheeses, like the feta cheese that is still made in Greece today. The Romans made soft cheeses too, but they also developed a way of making hard cheeses.

The Romans practiced their cheese-making skills in many parts of their empire. During the Roman period, farmers in France and Britain became very skilled at making cheese.

Family cows

In the Middle Ages (around 1000 to 1450 CE), people all over Europe kept dairy cows. Families often had their own cow to supply all their milk, butter, and cheese. The cow was milked by the women and children of the family.

This illustration shows how a butter churn from the Middle Ages worked.

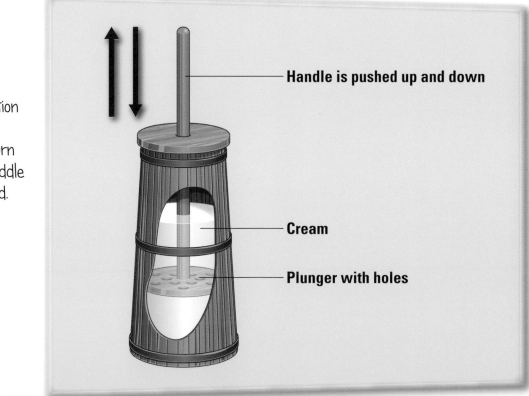

Handle is pushed up and down

Cream

Plunger with holes

Making butter at home

The woman of the house made the family's butter. First she skimmed off the cream that rose to the top of the milk. Then she used a wooden butter churn to turn the cream into butter. Simple butter churns are still used today in some parts of the world.

Early Butter Churn

For many centuries, people used a simple wooden churn to turn cream into butter. Cream was poured into a tall wooden barrel. Then a wooden plunger was pushed up and down inside the barrel to churn up the cream. The repeated movement of the plunger turned the liquid cream into solid butter.

Churning cream into butter was very hard work!

Dairy herds

By the 1700s, many towns and cities had grown throughout Europe, America, and Australia. People living in towns went to their local market to buy **dairy products**. Farmers in the country kept dairy herds, and their milk, cream, and cheese were taken to market by cart.

Parlors and dairies

Cows on farms were usually milked by women who were known as dairymaids or milkmaids. Milking took place in a building called a **milking parlor** (or a milking shed). Cream, butter, and cheese were produced in a cool room close to the milking parlor. This room was known as the dairy.

Gustaf de Laval (1845–1913)

The Swedish inventor Gustaf de Laval spent most of his life making improvements in dairy farming. In 1894 he designed a cream separator that made the job of separating cream from milk much easier and faster than before. The Laval separator was used all over the world.

Dairy breeds

Farmers kept special dairy cows that produced high-quality milk. Dairy breeds included Holsteins from the Netherlands, Ayrshires from Scotland, Brown Swiss from Switzerland, and Guernseys and Jerseys from the Channel Islands. When settlers arrived in North America, Australia, and New Zealand, they brought their dairy cows with them. The same basic breeds are kept in dairy farms all over the world.

The Laval separator worked by spinning milk very fast. The milk, which is heavier, was pulled outward against the walls of the separator. The cream, which is lighter, was collected in the middle. Then the cream and milk flowed out of separate spouts.

How Did Dairy Farms Develop?

By the 1850s, some farmers in Europe and the United States had started to **specialize** in dairy production. Instead of running a mixed farm with crops and animals, they had dairy farms with large herds of cows. But dairy farmers had to cope with some difficult challenges.

Dairy problems

Farmers with large herds faced the problem of storing large quantities of milk. Milk quickly turned sour, especially in hot weather. There was also the danger that milk could contain harmful **bacteria** (germs). People could catch diseases like tuberculosis (a very serious lung disease) by drinking the milk of unhealthy cows.

Dairy farmers worked hard to make their herds more **productive**. They tried feeding their cows a range of different grasses to see which food produced the best results.

Pasteurization

In 1862 Louis Pasteur discovered a method of treating milk by heating it and then cooling it quickly. This process was later called **pasteurization**. It makes milk last longer without turning sour and also makes it healthier to drink (see box). Pasteurization machines were first introduced in 1895. Almost all the milk that we buy today has been pasteurized. Unpasteurized milk is used to make some cheeses.

Louis Pasteur (1822–1895)

Louis Pasteur was a leading French chemist. He was one of the first scientists to recognize that all substances contain bacteria (germs). Pasteur realized that the bacteria in milk multiply very fast, causing milk to go "bad." He also discovered that most of these bacteria were destroyed when he heated milk. Heating milk also destroys many of the harmful germs that can cause illness. Pasteur's work saved many lives.

Pasteur did not only invent pasteurization. He also developed **vaccinations** to prevent the spread of deadly diseases.

Keeping cool

The process of pasteurization made milk last longer, but farmers still had the problem of keeping milk cold. This problem was not fully solved until the 1930s, when refrigerated tanks were introduced on farms.

Milking problems

As dairy farms grew in size, farmers struggled to milk all their cows. Cows had to be milked twice a day, and even experienced dairymaids could not milk more than six cows an hour. In the 19th century, many people tried to create a milking machine that copied the actions of the dairymaids. However, it was not until the 1920s that a really successful machine was invented.

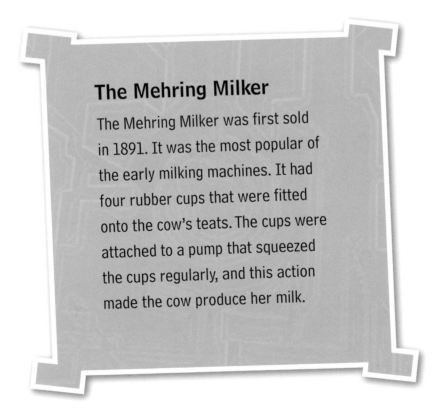

The Mehring Milker

The Mehring Milker was first sold in 1891. It was the most popular of the early milking machines. It had four rubber cups that were fitted onto the cow's teats. The cups were attached to a pump that squeezed the cups regularly, and this action made the cow produce her milk.

Dairy plants

By the 1940s, most dairy farmers had stopped making their own butter and cheese. Instead they sent their milk to a dairy **plant**, where the milk was treated and **processed** into other **dairy products**. The introduction of refrigerated tankers in the 1950s meant that ice-cold milk could be delivered directly from the farm to the dairy plant.

Traditional milking parlors, such as this one in the 19th century, began to change once machinery was introduced.

How Did Egg Production Begin?

Egg production began about 9,000 years ago when wild fowl were first tamed in China. Around the same time, hens were being raised in India. Over the next few thousand years, red jungle fowl from China and India were transported to many parts of Asia, Africa, and Europe. They are the ancestors of our modern egg-laying hens.

Which bird is best?

In ancient Egypt and China, people kept hens, geese, and ducks for their eggs. The practice of keeping hens began in Europe around 700 BCE, although goose eggs were also common in medieval Europe. In North America, American Indians kept wild turkeys for their meat and eggs, but when the early settlers arrived in America they brought their own hens from Europe. Gradually hens became the standard egg-laying bird all over the world.

Red jungle fowl still live in the wild in India and China.

Over the centuries, people developed special breeds of hens that were very good at laying eggs. In the United States, the single-comb white leghorn is a popular breed.

Eggs for the family

By the 1200s, many families kept hens of their own. Hens lay an egg every day or every two days, so a family with several hens could collect some eggs every day. When the hens became too old to lay eggs, they were killed and eaten.

In **developed countries**, such as the United States, the practice of keeping family hens gradually died out. By the 1800s, most families were buying their eggs from farmers. However, in many parts of the world, families still keep a few hens to supply all the eggs they need.

Larger flocks

Until the 1900s, farmers kept a small flock of hens as part of a mixed farm. The hens slept in wooden hen houses (sometimes known as coops) and **roamed** freely during the day. By the 1920s, however, farmers were keeping much larger flocks. Their hens spent most of their time inside large hen houses.

The method of egg production where hens are kept in cages is known as **factory farming** or "battery farming." It has been widely criticized because it causes a lot of stress to hens.

Crowded hens

Hens in crowded hen houses experienced a range of problems. They became panicky and pecked at each other. They fought each other for food, and some of them starved. They also developed diseases from standing in their own droppings.

Hens in cages

In the 1930s, farmers began to keep hens in wire cages. The cages stood on shelves inside huge sheds. The hens fed from a food trough. Their eggs rolled into a metal chute, and their droppings fell through the floor of their cage.

Keeping hens in cages cut down on some diseases, but the birds were still very crowded. (There were usually five hens in each cage.) They still pecked at each other, and they became very stressed and unhealthy.

In the 1960s, egg producers realized that hens produced more eggs when they were kept in constant light. So the lights in the laying sheds were never turned off. Farmers also started "debeaking" their hens to stop them from pecking at each other. This involved burning off the sharp part of the hens' beaks.

What Methods Are Used for Milking?

Modern dairy farmers rely on milking machines. These machines make the job of milking much easier and faster than in the past. Today's farmers can milk between 100 and 220 cows an hour.

Milking machines

Modern milking machines have four teat cups made from stainless steel with a soft rubber lining. The cups are linked by a "claw" that leads into a tube for collecting milk. Each teat cup also has a small air tube leading into it. The air tube is linked to a pump that creates a regular squeezing and releasing movement. This movement makes the cow release her milk.

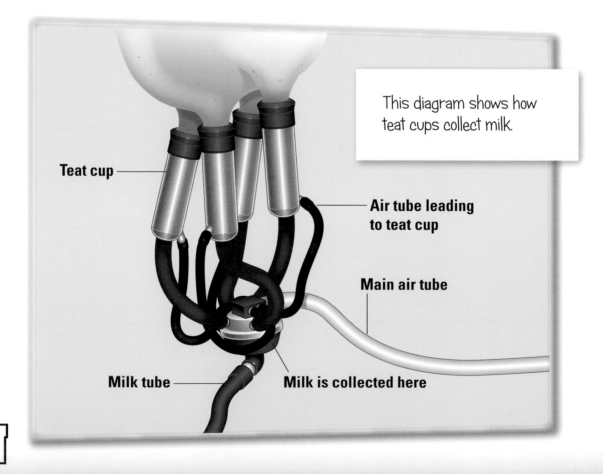

This diagram shows how teat cups collect milk.

Teat cup

Air tube leading to teat cup

Main air tube

Milk tube

Milk is collected here

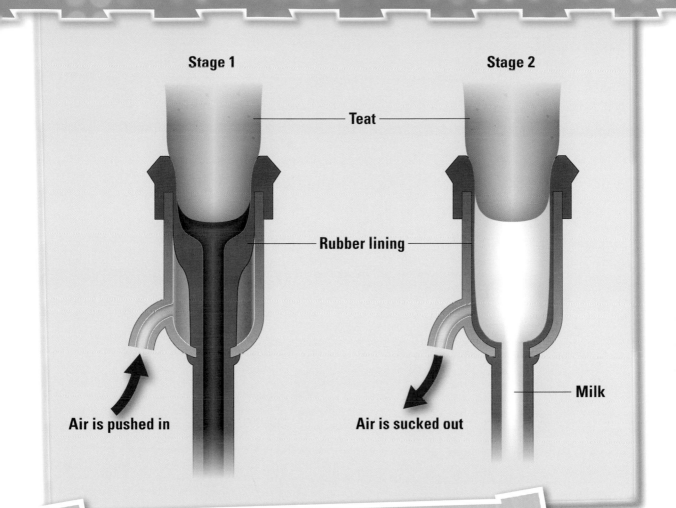

Stage 1

Stage 2

Teat

Rubber lining

Milk

Air is pushed in

Air is sucked out

How Does a Milking Machine Work?

A milking machine works in two stages. In stage one, the pump pushes air through the air tube into the teat cup. The rubber lining expands and gently squeezes the teat, but no milk flows. In stage two, the pump sucks air out. The rubber lining collapses and releases the pressure on the teat. The teat relaxes and opens, and milk flows into the milk tube.

Rotary parlors

In the 1980s, the first rotary parlors were introduced. In a rotary parlor, the cows are loaded one at a time onto a circular platform, which rotates very slowly. A dairy worker puts the cups on the cows as they move past. Then the milking machine does its work. By the time the platform has made a complete rotation, the cow has been milked. The cups are removed **automatically** and the cow's teats are sprayed with disinfectant. Then the cow steps off the platform and walks toward her feed.

Automatic Milking Systems

Over the last 30 years, some automatic milking systems (AMS) have been developed. In these systems, the cow decides when she wants to be milked. She walks toward an automatic gate, where a computer checks whether she has been recently milked. If the cow is allowed through the gate, she walks to a milking station (a place where she is milked). At the milking station, a **robotic arm** fits the milking machine onto the cow's teats. The cow is milked, the machine is removed, and the cow's teats are sprayed with disinfectant. All these processes are performed automatically.

Modern milking parlors

Modern **milking parlors** are designed to make milking as easy as possible. Cows enter the parlor through automatic gates, and dairy workers stand on sunken platforms so that they do not need to bend to reach the cows' teats.

Most rotary milking systems have places for around 40 cows. It is possible to milk up to 220 cows an hour using a rotary system.

How Are Milk and Cream Processed?

Milk and cream are usually **processed** at a dairy **plant** (factory). The first and most important process is **pasteurization**. This involves heating the milk to around 160°F (70°C) to make the milk last longer and to kill off harmful **bacteria**. Pasteurized milk can last up to three weeks if it is kept very cold.

UHT milk

Some milk is given a special heat treatment to make it last a very long time. This kind of milk is known as UHT milk or long-life milk. (The initials UHT stand for ultra-heat-treated.) UHT milk is heated to 275°F (135°C) for a short time to kill germs. If it is kept in a sealed container, it can last for up to nine months without being refrigerated.

Powdered milk

Some milk has all the moisture removed from it in order to produce powdered milk. Powdered milk is an **ingredient** in many factory-made foods, such as cakes and cookies. It is also used to make infant formula (milk for babies).

Cream and skim milk

Some of the milk in a dairy plant goes through a process to separate the cream from the milk. This is done in a large machine called a **centrifuge** (or spinner). After all the cream has been separated from the milk, a thin liquid called **skim milk** is left behind. People drink skim milk when they want to avoid fat in their diet.

Giant centrifuges (spinners) are used to separate cream from milk in a dairy plant. They work in the same way as the cream separator described on page 13.

Homogenized milk

If cream is not removed from milk, it forms a thick layer on the milk's surface. In the past people liked to have milk with cream on top. But now our milk is **homogenized**. This means the milk has gone through a process to spread the cream evenly throughout the milk (see page 29).

Semi-skimmed milk

Many people today like to drink semi-skimmed milk. To make semi-skimmed milk, a small proportion of cream is added back to skim milk. Then the cream is mixed up with the milk using the process of homogenization.

All sorts of cream

Cream is sold in a range of thicknesses, each with a different fat content. Heavy whipping cream, used in cooking, is about 36 percent fat. Half-and-half is a mixture of milk and cream with between 10.5 and 18 percent fat. Whole milk is between 3 and 4 percent fat. Ice cream is made by freezing cream slowly and adding a lot of sugar.

Unhomogenized milk (milk with large globules of cream)

Globules are squeezed

Globules are squeezed again

Homogenized milk (milk with small globules of cream)

How Does a Milk Homogenizer Work?

A milk homogenizer is a large metal container. Milk is poured into the homogenizer and forced at very high pressure through tiny spaces. This process breaks down the globules (drops) of cream in the milk and creates much smaller globules. The tiny globules of cream are no longer light enough to rise to the top of the milk, so they stay evenly spread throughout the milk.

How Are Other Dairy Foods Produced?

Butter is one of the best-selling dairy foods. It is made by churning (stirring it vigorously) cream until it forms a solid mass (see page 11). In modern dairy **plants**, cream is churned in huge metal containers. Sometimes vegetable oil is mixed with the butter to make it soft and easy to spread.

Curds and whey

Many dairy products are made from **fermented** milk. This is milk that has gone sour. When milk is fermented, it separates into two substances: solid **curds** and liquid **whey**. The curds are turned into cheese. Whey is often fed to farm animals.

Cottage cheese is made up of curds and whey. The lumps are tiny cheese curds and the liquid is whey. It has a mild flavor because the bacteria in the curds have not been left to ferment for long.

When cheese is in the soft, curd stage, it can be cut very easily.

Producing cheese

When milk is fermented to make cheese, a substance called **rennet** is added. This makes the curds more solid. The resulting cheese is soft and slightly rubbery. Some soft cheeses are finished at this stage.

Hard cheeses are heated to 95°F to 131°F (35°C to 55°C). The gentle heat removes more whey, but it does not destroy the **bacteria** in the cheese. The bacteria continue the fermenting process, creating a cheese with a strong, tangy flavor. Some cheeses are left to **mature** for a few weeks. Others take much longer. Parmesan cheese is matured for at least a year in order to gain its strong flavor.

All sorts of cheeses

There are hundreds of different cheeses, and they each have their own recipe. The makers of the Swiss cheese Emmentaler use special bacteria to ferment their curd. The bacteria produce large bubbles that leave holes in the cheese when it hardens. Dutch cheese-makers wash their curds in warm water to make them taste less tangy. This creates mild cheeses, like Edam or Gouda.

Cheese presses have been used for thousands of years. This one dates back to the 1800s.

Cheese Press

A cheese press is used to squeeze the last drops of moisture from a cheese. A heavy weight pushes down on the cheese, and liquid escapes through the bottom of the press.

While they are maturing, blue cheeses are pierced with needles to create tiny air holes. Air enters the cheese and helps the mold grow.

Mozzarella and blue cheese

The curd for mozzarella cheese is stretched and **kneaded** in hot water, rather like kneading dough to make bread. This makes the cheese stretchy and stringy when you cook it. Blue cheeses have a special mold added to them. As the mold develops, it turns a blue-green color and adds a very strong flavor to the cheese.

Making yogurt

Yogurt is made from fermented milk that has been heated. First the milk is heated to around 176°F (80°C). This prevents the milk from forming curds and whey. Then the milk is cooled to around 113°F (45°C). The milk is kept warm for four to seven hours while it ferments and turns into yogurt.

How Are Eggs Processed?

Today's egg producers usually collect their eggs as soon as they are laid. The eggs are placed on trays and stored in a cool place. Some large egg farms have their own **processing plants**. Others send their eggs to a processing plant in refrigerated trucks. At the plant the eggs are washed, checked, graded, and packed. Many of these processes are performed **automatically** by special machines.

Cleaning

When the eggs arrive at the plant, they are transferred to a **conveyor belt**. The belt carries the eggs through all the processing stages. The first stage is cleaning. The eggs are turned gently as brushes and water jets move carefully across them. Then a fan dries the eggs.

Rows of tiny suction cups gently lift up the eggs and place them on the conveyor belt. (The color of the eggs—brown or white— depends on the breed of hen that laid them.)

The process of checking eggs is called candling. In the past, eggs were checked by holding each one in front of a candle.

Checking

After the eggs have been cleaned, the conveyor belt carries them into a **candling** room. This is a darkened area with bright lights shining under the eggs. An experienced checker spots any eggs that are old or cracked. Old eggs have a thinner albumen (or egg "white") than fresh eggs. This makes the yolk look darker when a light is shone through the egg. Checkers also look for any unusual spots that could be a sign of disease.

Grading

At the candling stage, eggs are given the grades A, B, or C. The A-grade eggs are the best quality. They are sold to supermarkets. B-grade eggs are healthy and uncracked, but they are oddly shaped so they cannot be sold in stores. They are sent to factories to be used in cakes, cookies, and other foods. C-grade eggs are cracked or old and cannot be used for human food. They are sent to egg-breakers, who use their shells. Dried eggshells are used in animal feed and soil **fertilizers**.

Weighing

Once all the A-grade eggs have been selected, they are weighed by an automatic weighing machine. The machine sorts the eggs into different sizes according to their weight. In the United States, eggs can be extra large, large, medium, and small.

USDA

The United States Department of Agriculture (USDA) is responsible for checking the safety of food produced on American farms. USDA inspectors are sent to egg processing plants to check on all their processes. The inspectors make sure that the plants meet very high standards of **hygiene** and food safety.

Packing

After the eggs have been weighed, a packing machine places the eggs in the correct carton for their weight. Eggs may be packed in cardboard or **polystyrene** cartons. Then the cartons are stacked in trucks, ready to be sent out to the grocery store.

In the final stage of egg production, the eggs are packed into cartons. Throughout the production process, the eggs are never touched by human hands.

What Methods Do Organic Farmers Use?

During the last 20 years, there has been a growing interest in **organic farming**. Organic farmers aim to produce foods that are as natural as possible. They feed their animals food that is free from chemicals and allow them to **roam** outside.

Intensive or organic?

Today's dairy farmers have to make a choice between **intensive farming** or organic farming. Most dairy farmers in the United States choose to use very intensive methods.

Intensive dairy farmers feed their cows **high-protein** cereals to increase their milk production. Cows on intensive farms in the United States are also given **growth hormones** to make them produce more milk and **antibiotic** drugs to keep them free from diseases. (In other countries, cows are not given growth hormones.) A few intensive farmers practice **zero grazing**, which means keeping cows indoors for most of their lives. Some people believe that these practices have a bad effect on the cows' milk, but most people drink milk from cows that have been intensively farmed.

The Organic Consumers Association

The Organic Consumers Association (OCA) **campaigns** for healthier practices in farming. OCA members support farmers who produce chemical-free food, and they campaign for better treatment of farm animals. The OCA also encourages people to buy organic food from local farms.

Organic dairy farms

Cows on organic dairy farms feed on grass that has been grown without using chemicals. The cows are also fed some cereals, but these are chemical free. Organic farmers follow strict guidelines on what drugs they can use to treat sick cows.

Organic farmers claim that their dairy products are better for people's health.

Cruelty to hens?

Hens on **factory farms** are kept in very cramped conditions (see page 21). In recent years, some lawmakers have recognized this fact and have made some moves to **ban** factory farming. In 2008 California passed the Prevention of Farm Animal Cruelty Act. This bans the keeping of hens in spaces that are too small for them to stretch their wings. However, organizations like Compassion in World Farming (see page 41) say that hens should never be kept in cages.

Some egg farmers produce "barn eggs." These are not the same as free-range eggs, because the hens that produce them have to stay in their barn and cannot roam outside. In the United States, barn eggs are often described on the carton as "free-range" eggs.

Free-range hens

A growing number of farmers keep free-range hens. These hens are free to roam outside during the day. At night they sleep in barns with nesting boxes and perches.

Organic eggs

Organic eggs come from free-range hens that are fed entirely with organic food. During the day, the hens roam on land that has been farmed without the use of chemicals.

In the United States, cage-free eggs make up less than 10 percent of the total egg market, but this share is growing.

Compassion in World Farming

Compassion in World Farming aims to stop all cruelty to animals on farms in the United Kingdom. Its members campaign peacefully against cruel practices such as keeping hens in "factory" cages, and zero grazing for dairy cows. Compassion in World Farming also gives prizes to farmers who treat their animals with compassion (kindness).

What's the Future for Dairy and Egg Production?

Many dairy farmers and egg producers choose to run very large-scale, intensive farms with the help of modern **technology**. Some farmers in the United States keep herds of more than 15,000 cows. One American egg producer has a total of 26 million laying hens.

Going large

Most of the foods produced on large-scale farms are sold in supermarkets. But supermarkets are always trying to cut the price of food. This means the farmers are paid less for their products. Farmers today are under a lot of pressure to produce large quantities of food very cheaply.

Buying local

In some places, small-scale farmers avoid supermarkets completely. Instead they run farm shops or sell their products at farmers' markets. Food that is sold at a farmers' market is more likely to be organic. But buyers should always ask the farmers about their practices. Many people are happy to spend more money when they buy from local farmers. They feel that they can trust the farmers to produce healthy food that does not involve any cruelty to animals.

Small and special

A growing number of dairy farmers and egg producers have decided to run small-scale farms. These farmers often use **organic farming** methods. Some small-scale dairy farmers make their own brands of cheese or yogurt.

This farm has chosen to sell its free-range eggs at a farmers' market rather than a store.

Future choices

Today's farmers face a difficult choice. Should they run a large-scale farm, using **intensive farming** methods to produce enormous quantities of food? Or should they concentrate on producing smaller amounts of high-quality food? High-quality food is expensive to produce, but it can be sold at a higher price.

Glossary

antibiotic drug that is used to cure infections

automatic happening without human control

bacteria tiny cells that are found in all living things. Some bacteria are useful, but others cause diseases.

ban to forbid something

campaign to take action in support of something

candling process of checking eggs by shining a light though them

centrifuge machine that spins liquids around very fast

conveyor belt moving belt that carries objects through a factory

curds solid part of fermented milk, when it separates into curds and whey

dairy products milk and other foods that are made from milk

developed country country, such as the United States, that has many factories and uses high-level technology

factory farming type of farming where animals are kept in cages

fermented turned sour. When milk is turned into cheese, it is usually deliberately fermented by adding special bacteria to it.

fertilizer substance that is added to soil to make it richer

growth hormone drug that makes animals grow larger and stronger or produce more milk

high-protein very rich in protein. Proteins are needed by animals and humans to help their bodies grow and stay strong. High-protein foods help cows produce large amounts of milk.

homogenized processed so that the fat is spread evenly throughout a liquid

hygiene making sure that something is clean and free from germs

ingredient one of the items that is used to make a food

intensive farming farming that uses a lot of technology and chemicals in order to be as productive as possible

knead punch and stretch. Substances such as cheese curd and bread dough are kneaded to make them more elastic and springy.

mature to ripen and become stronger-tasting

milking parlor large building where cows are milked

organic farming farming that avoids all chemicals and aims to give farm animals a natural, healthy life

pasteurization heating milk to kill off some bacteria. Pasteurization makes milk last longer without turning sour, and it kills off some of the germs that spread diseases.

plant factory where dairy products or eggs are processed

polystyrene light, stiff plastic that is often used for packaging

processed treated and changed in some way. Milk is processed into butter and cheese.

productive able to produce more or make more

react to change in some way when mixed with another substance

rennet substance found in the stomach of cows that helps to separate milk into solid curds and liquid whey

roam to move around freely

robotic arm arm that is controlled by a computer

skimmed milk milk with almost all its fat removed

specialize concentrate on one skill

technology use of machinery and computers to do practical jobs

vaccination injection that prevents people from catching a disease

whey watery part of fermented milk, when it separates into curds and whey

zero grazing practice of keeping animals indoors and not allowing them to roam and eat outside

Find Out More

Books

Bailey, Gerry. *Farming for the Future*. New York: Gareth Stevens, 2011.

Fandel, Jennifer. *Louis Pasteur and Pasteurization*. Mankato, Minn.: Capstone, 2010.

Peterson, Cris. *Clarabelle: Making Milk and So Much More*. Honesdale, Pa.: Boyds Mill Press, 2007.

Vogel, Julia. *Local Farms and Sustainable Foods*. Ann Arbor, Mich.: Cherry Lake, 2010.

Wolfman, Judy. *Life on a Dairy Farm*. Minneapolis, Minn.: Carolrhoda Books, 2006.

Websites

Dairy Farming Today
Dairy Farming Today is a website run by the American Dairy Association. You can find information on dairy farming with videos. The site includes sections on "Life on the Farm," "Quality and Safety," and "Myth versus Fact." You can also take a virtual tour of a dairy farm. This site represents large, high-tech farms.

www.dairyfarmingtoday.org/Pages/Home.aspx

Department of Agriculture (USDA)
This site on egg production from the United States Department of Agriculture (USDA) discusses egg and other food safety and provides answers to a list of frequently asked questions.

www.fsis.usda.gov/factsheets/focus_on_shell_eggs/index.asp

Organic Consumers Association (OCA)
This is the website of the Organic Consumers Association (OCA), which operates in the United States and Canada. The site explains the aims of the OCA and provides information and news on organic farmers and farming practices. You can read reports of the latest OCA campaigns and find a list of organic events for each state.

www.organicconsumers.org/

Dairy Council of California

This website is run by the Dairy Council of California. You can find many dairy facts and learn more about a healthy diet, types of milk, and dairy shopping tips.

http://www.dairycouncilofca.org/Milk-Dairy/Facts.aspx

Places to visit

Farm Visits

You can find organic farms to visit by typing "farm visit" into the search box of The Organic Consumers Association website.

www.organicconsumers.org

Museums

There are many local museums of rural life that give you a good idea of farming practices in the past. You can find your nearest museum by searching on the Internet.

www.outdoorhistory.org/

Farmers' Markets

Use the website below to find a farmers' market near you. At many farmers' markets, you can speak with farmers who might be able to tell you more about their farming practices.

http://search.ams.usda.gov/farmersmarkets/

Agricultural Shows

A great way to see farm animals and all the latest farm machinery is to visit an agricultural show. State fairs often have livestock competitions and other agricultural events as well. Check on the Internet to find a show near you that welcomes visitors.

Index